Your
Leadership
Legacy

Your Leadership Legacy

◇

THE DIFFERENCE YOU MAKE
IN PEOPLE'S LIVES

Marta Brooks, Julie Stark,
Sarah Caverhill

BERRETT-KOEHLER PUBLISHERS, INC.
San Francisco

Berrett-Koehler Publishers, Inc.
235 Montgomery Street, Suite 650
San Francisco, CA 94104-2916
Tel: (415) 288-0260   Fax: (415) 362-2512   www.bkconnection.com

ORDERING INFORMATION
Quantity sales. Special discounts are available on quantity purchases by corporations, associations, and others. For details, contact the "Special Sales Department" at the Berrett-Koehler address above.

Individual sales. Berrett-Koehler publications are available through most bookstores. They can also be ordered directly from Berrett-Koehler:
Tel: (800) 929-2929; Fax: (802) 864-7626; www.bkconnection.com.

Orders for college textbook/course adoption use. Please contact Berrett-Koehler: Tel: (800) 929-2929; Fax: (802) 864-7626.

Orders by U.S. trade bookstores and wholesalers. Please contact Publishers Group West, 1700 Fourth Street, Berkeley, CA 94710. Tel: (510) 528-1444; Fax: (510) 528-3444.

Berrett-Koehler and the BK logo are registered trademarks of Berrett-Koehler Publishers, Inc.

Printed in the United States of America

Berrett-Koehler books are printed on long-lasting acid-free paper. When it is available, we choose paper that has been manufactured by environmentally responsible processes. These may include using trees grown in sustainable forests, incorporating recycled paper, minimizing chlorine in bleaching, or recycling the energy produced at the paper mill.

Copyediting and proofreading by PeopleSpeak. Design and composition by Beverly Butterfield, Girl of the West Productions.

Library of Congress Cataloging-in-Publication Data
Brooks, Marta, 1954-
   Your leadership legacy: the difference you make in people's lives / by
Marta Brooks, Julie Start, Sarah Caverhill.
     p. cm.
   ISBN 1-57675-287-9
   1. Leadership. 2. Interpersonal relations. 3. Organizational effectiveness.
I. Stark, Julie, 1960- II. Caverhill, Sarah, 1958- III. Title
HD57.7.B763 2004
658.4'092—dc22   2003063881

FIRST EDITION
09 08 07 06 05 04   10 9 8 7 6 5 4 3 2 1

CONTENTS

v

FOREWORD

In my life, I have always been concerned about the awe-some responsibility I feel to the people who work in our company and the clients we have, as well as my friends and family. I hope and pray that I have made or will make a positive difference in their lives.

I ask people all the time if they would like to leave the world a better place for their having been here. Everyone smiles and says, "Sure I would." Then I ask them, "What is your plan to do that?" Nine out of ten people laugh because they obviously don't have a plan. Yet we *all* can make the world a better place by the moment-to-moment decisions we make as we interact with others.

I believe that every passing moment in our lives is just another opportunity to make a positive difference in the lives of others. Whether we are sitting beside someone in an airplane, stepping onto an elevator with a stranger, or sitting in a company meeting, these are the very moments when we can give the gift of ourselves.

There is nothing fancy here. Regardless of our status, achievement, or position, our impact lies squarely on how we spend these moments—what we say and how we say it when we are with people and how they feel when we are gone. This is our "leadership legacy."

When I first read *Your Leadership Legacy*, I realized that whether we try or not, we will all have a leadership legacy. The question is, what kind of legacy will it be?

I think Marta Brooks, Julie Stark, and Sarah Caverhill have nailed it in describing the key ingredients that go into a positive leadership legacy. It starts with understanding that it's not about your position; it's who you are as a person that leaves a positive leadership legacy. My father was my teacher here. When I was in the seventh grade, I was elected president of my class. I came home all excited about sharing the good news with my parents. After congratulating me, my father said, "Ken, now that you are president and have a position, never use it. Great leaders are not effective because of the position they hold but because they are trusted and respected by others."

That leads to the second key ingredient—focusing on the people you are attempting to influence. After all, they are the key to getting anything done. That means you have to connect with them. My mother used to tell me, "Don't act like you are better than anyone else. But don't let anyone else act like they are better than you."

The final ingredient is driving your dream. My wife, Margie, always says, "A goal is a dream with a deadline." Leadership is about going somewhere. If you don't know where you are going, your leadership doesn't matter. A clear vision and direction gets people into the act of forgetting about themselves.

I am thrilled to have Marta, Julie, and Sarah and their book, *Your Leadership Legacy*, as part of the Ken Blanchard series at Berrett-Koehler. I have known Marta and Sarah for a long time. They have been two of our most outstanding consulting partners, spreading the good word about leading at a higher level to companies and organizations all over the country. Recently, Sarah became a sales leader and is already making an impact there. By joining up with their colleague Julie Stark, they have created a very special book with an important message.

If you care about what your leadership legacy looks like and want to shape it into an inspirational gift to others, you'll read this book.

The legacy you live is the legacy you leave.

KEN BLANCHARD
Coauthor of *The One Minute Manager*®

PREFACE

This book was born out of one simple question: What makes a person unforgettable? As management training and leadership professionals, as neighbors, parents, and friends, we spent five years talking one-on-one with hundreds of men and women. In conversations with leaders of companies included in *Fortune's 100 Best Companies to Work For* and in chance meetings on the corner, we asked, "Who left an indelible impression on you at work or in your personal life?" "Whose shoes would you walk in today if you could?" And most important, *"Why?"*

Our respondents were as varied as the walks of life you can imagine. The "why," however, was remarkably consistent. The people they described all had one thing in common. They all had personal and compelling character.

Our journey began in finding out what these memorable people were *doing* to make their impact timeless. And here's what we discovered. Regardless of their age, gender, or vocation, these people positively influenced change in the lives of those around them. They were engaged in a most unique and personal act of leadership.

What, then, is a leadership legacy? Your leadership legacy is the sum total of the difference you make in people's lives, directly and indirectly, formally and informally. The way you behave in your day-to-day life defines your legacy. The challenge is how to live in a way that creates a legacy others want to be a part of, too.

A great legacy doesn't just happen. Your legacy is built moment by moment, in small interactions. How you live your legacy can uplift people's spirits and inspire them to live or perform better than they thought possible. Or it can drag them down and create the opposite effect.

You will learn along with Doug, the main character, to adopt specific behaviors to change your legacy into one you are proud to leave. Through the modeling of some surprising mentors, you will witness courageous leaders who **Dare to Be a Person, Not a Position; Dare to Connect with People;** and **Dare to Drive the Dream.**

You may never know the full impact of your willingness to dare, but someone, and quite possibly *many someones*, will! Learn about the difference you make in people's lives. Dare to transform *Your Leadership Legacy*.

MARTA BROOKS
JULIE STARK
SARAH CAVERHILL
January 2004

chapter one

THE READING
OF THE WILL

Doug Roman was not in the mood for stop-and-go traffic.

"Obnoxious music," he snapped as he poked one of the buttons on the dash panel. The perfectly balanced sound of his custom audio system immediately replaced the cackling broadcast.

"Calm down, Doug," he told himself. "You've got plenty of time."

The reading of Nan's will was set for ten o'clock; by noon he would be the new CEO of Mooseland Stoneware. His aunt Nan had been more than an intelligent woman and the influential founder and CEO of Mooseland, the most prestigious stoneware company in the world. She had also been the single most important person in his life.

Doug glanced at his reflection in the rearview mirror.

"You've grown up to be a very handsome man," she'd told him often. "But that isn't why I love you."

1

Nan had taken full responsibility for him from the moment her doorbell had rung that rainy night those thirty-some years ago. The officer standing on her porch had explained how two young lives had been extinguished on a winding country road, the tragic result of the driver swerving to avoid a deer. In the midst of shock and grief, Nan had experienced a wave of relief, knowing that her younger brother's two-year-old son was sleeping safely in the guest room upstairs.

He had depended on her for everything. She was the one person in the world whom he had most loved and admired. And now she was gone. He knew that the reading of her will would mean that it was final.

Nan, why did you have to leave me?

He was late when he burst into the plush law offices of McCann & Pherson.

"Good afternoon, Mr. Roman," Tommy McCann's secretary said cheerfully as Doug breezed by her and pushed open the door to Tommy's inner office. He took a seat in the corner of the room so he could observe his relatives and the three board members who had gathered for the reading of the will.

Without addressing Doug directly, Tommy glanced over his half-glasses and cleared his throat. "I believe we are all present now. We are here to read the last will and testament of Nannette Mae Roman, executed . . . "

Nan had updated her will less than three months ago. Had she had a premonition that she was going to die? Why hadn't she said anything to me?

Tommy read name after name followed by the gifts that Nan had painstakingly selected for each one. It was clear that Nan had been generous, too generous in Doug's estimation, with his cousins and their families. She had also designated impressive gifts for some of her employees, friends, and favorite charities.

When is Tommy going to get to my name?

"I'm going to ask everyone but Doug and the board members to leave the room now." He waited while Doug's relatives filed out of the room, not one of them giving Doug any more than a side-glance.

When the door finally closed, Doug leaned forward in his chair. "All right, what's going on?"

Tommy handed Doug a shallow rectangular box. "Your aunt asked me to give this to you."

Inside the box was a bonded-leather book. There was no title, just the raised design of a fern in the upper right corner of the cover. Doug lifted the book out of the box. A letter was folded inside the book and the inside front cover contained an inscription in Nan's familiar handwriting:

Dearest Doug,
As your journey reveals the truth, write it. As the truth reveals your legacy, live it.
Love,
Nan

Doug felt a distinct tightness in his chest. Without looking up, he unfolded the letter.

My dearest Doug,
As I write this, I can't help but think how much I love you. I am so proud of the wonderful man you have become. All my remaining personal belongings shall be yours to do with as you wish. In addition, I bequeath to you all assets not otherwise cited in my will. Tommy will handle the necessary details.

Mooseland Stoneware, my most precious gift, is, of course, rightfully yours. You shall be the CEO and chairman six months from today with one stipulation—the board must vote unanimously that you have discovered the personal imperatives that will prepare you to live your leadership legacy. Doug, you and Mooseland mean so much to me. Though I suspect you are stunned by this letter, I could never want anything less than what is best for you and the company.

Therefore, it is my decision that you shall embark on a journey, one that will reveal unexplored gifts that you might not know you have. Be assured, my darling Doug, that wherever you find new truths about your legacy, I am cheering your discovery.

Every journey begins with one step. This card will help you get started.

May God bless you on your journey.

Love,

Nan

A business card with a picture of a fern embossed in the upper right corner and the name and address of a local garden center was clipped to the bottom of the page.

Doug looked up at Tommy. "Did you know about this?"

"Yes, I did. Nan and I were colleagues and friends for many years. She and I discussed her plans at length, though I must say this is happening much sooner than she thought it would. The board members have received copies of this letter and another letter of instruction from your aunt. The second letter explains their responsibility to render a decision six months from today regarding your competence to serve as Mooseland's leader."

What was Nan talking about? Am I destined to be forever burdened with her ideas about leadership? Any doubts as to my achievements and suitability to lead Mooseland could be dispelled with a glance at my resume. And what am I supposed to do with this business card?

"This has to be some kind of mistake. What is my leadership legacy?"

"No, Doug, there's no mistake."

Doug stared at Tommy, waiting for an explanation.

"Building a leadership legacy differs from building a resume. A person's resume may include pages of experience and accomplishments. But none of that reflects that person's suitability to serve as a leader.

"Nan believed that the legacy you live is the legacy you leave. Do you have any sense of *your* leadership legacy? She was saying that if you're going to take the top leadership position of Mooseland, you must discover what it takes to live your leadership legacy. She knew what she was talking about. Trust her."

Doug looked down at the letter and then up at Tommy. "This is nuts. All of you are completely out of your minds!"

With that, he got up and left.

After Doug's abrupt departure, Tommy again addressed the board. "It is important that you understand the task Nan has set before you. Nan's dream is that Doug will master three crucial imperatives of effective leadership and begin to live his leadership legacy. Within six months, you must be convinced that he is willing to Dare to Be a Person, Not a Position; Dare to Connect with People; and Dare to Drive the Dream."

chapter two

EVERY JOURNEY
BEGINS WITH
ONE STEP

Driving away from Tommy's office was a blur for Doug. *What just happened? Why would Nan, whom I trusted and loved more than anyone else, do this to me? How am I supposed to discover my leadership legacy?*

"I'll quit, that's what I'll do. I love Mooseland but I don't have to work there." Even as he said these words, he knew they were hollow. He cared about Mooseland and he wanted to do right by Nan, but what was she asking him to do?

As Doug zoomed past the manicured streetscape, his thoughts softened a bit as he remembered happier days. "My, aren't you full of yourself," Nan had teased, "but I love you just the same." On other occasions, he would carry on about a mistake *this* person had made or a crazy idea that *that* person had proposed, and she would simply give him a loving pat on the cheek. In more serious moments, like the one a few weeks earlier, she had responded to one of his tirades with a tone that still disarmed him. "I love you," she had said softly, "not only for the person you are but for the person I know you'll become."

Returning to the present, he glanced at the empty journal flung carelessly on the seat beside him. His thoughts returned to the letter and the journey that Nan had planned for him. "Nan," he said aloud, "my leadership legacy? What is this all about?"

Truth Seekers Garden Center

Doug liked to solve problems with immediate action. If this was what Nan wanted, then so be it. It was Friday. He could handle a few items at the office, pick up his dry cleaning, and check out the garden center on the way home.

The sun was beginning to set as he approached the garden center. He found it easily and stopped safely away from other parked vehicles. Doug was not about to subject his car's flawless exterior to the assault of carelessly opened doors and recklessly piloted shopping carts.

The Truth Seekers Garden Center was busy as veteran landscapers and novice gardeners filled baskets and carts, intent on beautifying some corner of the world. Rows of perennials, annuals, and hanging baskets ready for adoption boasted all the rainbow's colors.

As Doug walked through the outside displays, pungent scents of soil, cedar mulch, and blooms engulfed him. He turned and looked at the panorama surrounding the garden center. There was a magnificence here that he had not noticed when he first pulled into the parking lot. Nan had loved the beauty of this part of the country and had often said that once she'd seen it, she knew she had found her new home. Perhaps it was this very view that had welcomed her so many years ago. Realizing he had heard Nan tell her stories for the last time, Doug's mood melted into sadness.

He made his way around the browsers and eventually found the entrance to the main building, recessed behind protective Victorian-style brick arches. As he came closer to the heart of the nursery, he overheard a young couple discussing their future. *What about me? What does this place have to do with me and my future as a leader and CEO?* At the main counter, he reached into his pocket and withdrew the business card. He studied the name printed on it: "Adoi, Master Gardener."

"May I help you?"

Doug found himself facing a woman with chocolate-colored skin holding a large fern, similar to the fern imprinted on the business card.

"I'm looking for Adoi," Doug said.

The woman smiled. "I am Adoi. I have been expecting you, Doug."

His mouth opened but, uncharacteristically, no words escaped.

Adoi smiled but said nothing.

"How did you know . . . ?" he asked slowly.

"I feel as if I know you."

Doug felt his head swimming. He wanted to turn and run. *From what? Adoi? The Truth Seekers Garden Center? What kind of name is that for a garden center?*

"Please follow me," Adoi said. He followed her as she walked leisurely along the path, deeper and deeper into what seemed to Doug to be a mysterious paradise.

Adoi remained quiet as she led the way. *Why am I following this woman? What does she have to do with Nan's journey assignment? Is she some kind of leadership legacy tour guide?*

As if reading his thoughts, Adoi stopped and turned to Doug. "I knew your aunt Nan. She was a wonderful woman," she said quietly. "I'm sorry for your loss. It is very difficult to say good-bye to someone who was so central in your life." Doug thought he noticed a tinge of sadness as she spoke. Her next words brought him up short. "Her legacy to all who knew her is so positive, so admirable."

Doug was about to reply, but Adoi had already turned and begun to walk again. *It sounds like Adoi had been close with Nan, yet I know nothing of her or of this garden center. This is crazy.*

She went around a display of plants depicting a high-country meadow and then passed through a wrought iron gate that was partially hidden by thick greenery. As he approached the gate, he noticed an engraved plate affixed to the ornamental iron. A fern was etched into an upper corner of the plate that read "Welcome Truth Seekers."

But it was the appearance of Nan's phrase below that numbed Doug: "Every journey begins with one step."

Adoi led him to a pavilion situated in a clearing where several paths converged. At the center of the pavilion were an ornate wrought iron table and two chairs. Adoi took a seat and motioned to Doug to do the same.

Doug began to sit but then stopped. He eyed the iced tea pitcher resting on the table. A beautiful, signature moose from Mooseland Stoneware adorned the distinctive pitcher and the mugs waiting to be filled. He raised his eyes and saw that Adoi was watching him. "I don't understand." Even before he finished the sentence, he noticed other Mooseland pieces. Bird feeders graced the branches of the old oak tree, and whimsical garden creatures hung from trellises and pillars overrun with climbing roses and ivy.

Why wasn't I aware of this place? They must be a large account.

"Please sit down," Adoi said as she again motioned to the empty chair.

Doug nodded and eased himself down into the chair as Adoi poured iced tea into the mugs.

"Back there, you said you knew Nan and that you've been expecting me. How is that possible?"

"Your aunt was a gifted gardener. She came by nearly every week to nurture this garden. Over the past few years, we became good friends."

Doug looked around. "This garden? I didn't realize."

"You know that Nan loved gardening, right?"

He nodded. Of course he knew. Whenever she had a moment of free time, she was outside, working in her garden. The garden event center and offices of Mooseland were proof positive of Nan's green thumb.

"I've been expecting you because of your aunt's letter."

"You know about the letter? First Tommy and now you. Did everyone know about the letter but me?"

"Those of us who loved your aunt knew. But not because she betrayed any trust. Your aunt would never have done such a thing."

"I know that," he said guardedly.

"We could never have known Nan without knowing you—you were such a vital part of her life—even if you did not know us."

"Yeah, well that doesn't explain much," Doug replied. "What is it that Nan wants from me? Will I discover my leadership legacy from you? Is that why I'm here?"

"Perhaps it is what your aunt wants *for* you," Adoi suggested gently. "Nan lived her leadership legacy. She always hoped you would do the same."

"Why would I worry about living my leadership legacy when I had not been given a leadership role? Nan was the leader. My job was to crunch numbers."

"Perhaps your definition of leadership is a bit narrow."

Doug felt a pang of resentment at Adoi's comment. *What right does she have to counsel me? We've known each other less than an hour. She's what? Maybe ten years older than me? She's a gardener. What qualifies her as an authority on Nan or my leadership legacy?*

"Look, I thought Nan wanted success for me. I thought she wanted me to take over Mooseland. If you know about the letter, then you know there's a hitch. I have six months to accomplish Nan's mission of constructing a leadership legacy. Why do I need a leadership legacy? Aren't legacies for old people? I have no idea what I'm supposed to do. Your business card was attached to Nan's letter. So, I took 'one step in my so-called journey' and here I am."

They sat silently for several moments. Finally, Doug spoke. "No secret leadership legacy formula? No words of truth?"

"Words of truth," Adoi's voice mimicked Doug's inflection, but, unlike his voice, Adoi's tone was calm. "You know, the truth is, Nan had exceptional abilities. All these trees and plants you see here benefited from her guidance. She paid attention to them and learned the best way to nourish each one."

Doug shook his head. "I agree that Nan was a great gardener. What is the point?"

"Living things are not carbon copies of one another," Adoi continued. "One regimen of care does not benefit all plants; soil, light, moisture, and temperature must be tailored to each plant's specific needs. Some living things survive in extraordinary circumstances, but if our goal is to thrive and to encourage those around us to thrive, we must consider individual needs. Would you treat an oak tree like you would treat a rose?"

"I am sure that your intention is to help me. But—"

"Your aunt had a special affection for this oak tree," Adoi said, rising and gesturing toward a large tree to Doug's left. "She regarded it as majestic yet humble because it provides shelter for some of nature's more fragile creations, allowing them to mature and thrive. Nan was strong and powerful, yet she constantly found ways to attend to those around her so that they, too, could blossom.

"I believe her understanding of nature was a model for her approach to life. For example, perhaps you can appreciate the good fortune of an orphaned infant who was blessed with a loving relative, one who provided him sanctuary and dedicated her life to nurturing his."

"I know what my aunt did for me," Doug said impatiently. "But what does Nan's green thumb and her affection for an oak tree have to do with my leadership legacy and becoming CEO of Mooseland?"

"I think Nan would be impressed by your question. Indeed, what do a CEO and a master gardener have in common?"

"Am I supposed to take up gardening to find out?"

Adoi fingered a nearby fern. "Isn't this plant beautiful?" she asked. "Healthy and thriving."

"Yes, it's a very nice plant," Doug answered in a patronizing voice. "Beyond that, I'm afraid I'm not much of a horticulture expert. As you've pointed out, Nan was the plant aficionado in our family."

Adoi persisted. "Come closer and tell me what you see."

Doug decided the quickest way to finish this meeting was to do as Adoi asked. Rising and stepping toward the plant, Doug said, "Well, it's green and it appears to be some kind of fern."

"That's a good start. This is a *Microlepia strigosa*," Adoi said as she gently misted the fronds with a hand sprayer. "This is just one of thousands of species of ferns in the world today. What else do you notice?"

"I'm not sure what you mean," Doug replied.

"Different plants require different environments to thrive. Tell me about this plant's environment. What do you notice about the soil and light? Go ahead, touch it. I promise you it is not poisonous."

"Okay, I'll play," Doug began, shaking his head. "The soil is moist and breaks apart easily." Surveying the surroundings, he added, "The fern is mostly in shade. There's a lot of breeze out there," he said, pointing to the screened outer walls, "but it is sheltered back here." Pleased with himself, Doug turned to Adoi. "Is that what you were looking for?"

"Not bad for your first time. Perhaps you are more of a plant aficionado than you realize," Adoi complimented him with a friendly smile. "You paused long enough from your busy schedule and used your senses to observe another living thing's growth."

Doug was unprepared for what happened next. Lifting it from its safe haven, Adoi placed the cumbersome planter containing the fern in Doug's hands. Not giving him a chance to refuse the gift, Adoi stated, "With you as its caretaker, this plant will continue to thrive because you know what it needs to flourish."

Looking at Adoi through the fronds that partially covered his face, Doug protested. "Adoi, you must be joking. I can't take this plant. I have never cared for plants, and I don't know the first thing about them. Trust me, this plant means more to you than it does to me. You can't seriously think I can keep this thing alive!"

Adoi moved to another fern and began tending to that one as she had the previous one. "You are right that I have enjoyed watching that fern grow for many years. But it will live with you now."

"Adoi, really . . ." Doug was trying to balance the unwieldy pot and follow Adoi.

"Sometimes, Doug, we become caretakers unexpectedly. Unforeseen circumstances place us in a position to be responsible for people and things that were once lovingly tended by another."

Adoi turned and faced Doug, then sealed the terms of their arrangement. "Declining or evading such a responsibility is not an option. Instead, our duty is to provide an environment that ensures the continued growth of that which has been entrusted to us. You have six months before the board meeting. Mooseland Stoneware will flourish under the leadership of someone who understands this: A large part of gardening is figuring out what you want to grow and providing an environment that is conducive to that growth.

"Sometimes we must observe how others have achieved goals that mirror our own. There is someone you should meet." Adoi drew a business card from her pocket and handed it to Doug.

She turned and started to leave but paused long enough to declare a challenge. "The next CEO of Mooseland Stoneware will become its leader and the custodian of its future—an enviable yet momentous responsibility. I hope that such a person would not be bested by a potted fern."

Doug noticed at once that the image of a fern was embossed in the upper right corner of the card. While he read it, Adoi departed through a screen door. Their meeting was over.

chapter three

THE FERN IS AS
GOOD AS DEAD

Doug was still annoyed later that evening when Elliott Stein, his friend and neighbor, stopped by after work. They had met several years earlier when they moved into neighboring townhomes. They were about the same age, and they both loved sports. When Doug wasn't too busy with Mooseland business and Elliott got a break from his CPA workload, they spent hours yelling at Doug's big screen over scored points, missed attempts, and bad calls.

"I've only got a few minutes, but I thought I'd see if you were popping the champagne, Mr. CEO."

Doug had noticed that since Nan's death, Elliott had come around a few times to say hello and see if he needed anything. During one of those visits, Doug had mentioned the upcoming meeting at Tommy's. "It's just a formality," he had told Elliott confidently. "I didn't think I'd be a CEO this early in life, but I'm ready."

As it turned out, it hadn't been just a formality.

"You won't believe what happened," Doug exclaimed as he grabbed a couple of microbrews from the refrigerator and headed toward the atrium patio. Elliott listened as Doug began a resentful account of the day. "First, it was my relatives. I can't believe what she gave to them. And get a load of this." Doug held up the journal he had begun scribbling in.

"What is it?" Elliott asked.

"It's a journal from Nan. She wants me to record truths revealed during my leadership legacy journey. This letter explains it." Doug handed the journal and Nan's letter to Elliott. "The board is going to decide if I have what it takes. Why would she do this?"

Elliott read the journal inscription and scanned the letter. "I'm sorry things didn't go like you thought they would. I spoke with Nan a lot that weekend we moved in. I have no doubt that she was proud of you. I think she was your biggest fan."

"Funny way to show it. Nan always had these weird ideas about sending me away to do things so I would learn something by doing them. Yak riding. White water rafting . . ."

"She sent you yak riding?" Elliott asked, laughing.

"No, but she might just as well have," Doug muttered. "I don't get it."

"Sounds like she wanted you to have the best the world has to offer. Let me ask you, did you dive into the experiences Nan arranged, or did you view those adventures as tasks on a checklist?"

"You know how it is. A successful business can't be built by someone who's not at work. I figured she wanted me to have little breaks here and there so I could come back fresh and ready to go."

"Knowing Nan, I suspect she had a little more than R&R in mind for you. Maybe your adventures were designed with another purpose in mind, some personal or professional growth perhaps? Have you ever thought about the differences between a journey and a vacation?"

"No, I guess not," Doug answered.

"When you take a vacation, you know when it starts and when it's over. There's a sense of putting your everyday life on hold and ignoring it for a while, but your intention is to return to where you started. With a journey, there's no predetermined destination or time frame and your everyday life is part of the trip. The focus is more on what you do along the way. Could it be that those adventures were Nan's way of attempting to jump-start a journey for you?"

Doug looked up at Elliott. He couldn't disagree.

"It sounds like your future—and Mooseland's future, for that matter—depends on your willingness to go along with her journey request."

"How will the board know what I've done to comply with her request? Will they take turns trailing me over the next six months? It sounds far-fetched."

"Nan obviously thought this was important enough to wager some pretty big chips. I don't believe she would have done this if she didn't have confidence in you and the board."

Doug shrugged.

"The journal seems like a good idea," Elliott added.

"Why?"

"Who knows? Later on you might enjoy reminiscing

about 'the early days,'" he said, grinning. Then, more seriously, he added, "Nan's inscription says that you are to write 'the truth.'"

"Yeah, look at page 1 and you'll see the truth."

Elliott read Doug's scrawled words.

Doug's Journal

I do not know what to write except that I think the idea of keeping this journal is crap. I have no idea what a leadership legacy is, I have no idea how people would remember me if I left this Earth today, and I don't care.

Elliott appeared to be amused by Doug's words. "Well, it's a start." As Elliott got up to leave, he glanced at the fern perched precariously on the counter in the dark and windowless butler's pantry. "I saw that fern on the way in and wondered where you got it. I was pretty sure you hated that kind of thing."

"Definitely not my idea," Doug sulked.

"Well, if you decide to spare its life, you might want to move it to a spot where it will get a little bit of light. Just a thought."

"I'll take that under advisement," said Doug absently.

After Elliott left, Doug picked up the journal and replayed the day's images for the hundredth time, hoping to be struck by a bolt of understanding. Nan. Tommy. Adoi. The board. His relatives.

"Don't be so hard on them," Nan had told him once after he'd complained about his cousins. "People tend to do the best they can with what they have. They are decent people. They do try."

"Try? They're horrible, Nan."

She had smiled at him. "Maybe it's not that they're so horrible but that you haven't taken the time to really understand them," she had said.

"How is it that every time I criticize someone you turn it around so it's me that's being criticized?" he had asked.

"Just be the man you're capable of being. You know what I mean."

He wanted to be the man she thought he could be. But, in truth, he often didn't know what she meant. Frankly, he thought he was becoming the man she envisioned. Hadn't he put in his time learning?

He had swept the shop floors, worked at the kiln, delivered mail, typed, and filed. If he ever expressed frustration or impatience while working those mundane jobs, she silenced him quickly.

"I want you to understand what it means to work, Doug. I want you to understand what this place means to the people who dedicate their time and energy to its success— not just what it means to you and me, the ones who benefit most from its financial rewards and its good name."

Nan had been relentless in seeking ways to make sure he learned "life lessons."

"Doug, you will take over Mooseland one day. Your success and Mooseland's success will depend on your understanding what I'm trying to teach you. You've got to take me seriously."

He had rolled his eyes. "Not another lecture," he had moaned good-naturedly. "Besides, I'm at the top of my class at college. I'll be ready."

"Darling, you need to be so much more than what you're learning in school. One of these days, I might decide to retire and Mooseland will need a new leader. Your education and your experience do not ensure your leadership capability."

"Okay, okay," he'd said, seeing how adamant she was. But he'd said it only to pacify her.

Doug would always remember Nan as a no-nonsense sort of woman. People were dealt all sorts of hardships, but she was determined to meet life head-on with character, no matter the circumstance. Development of character, in her mind, required challenges and adventures. While his friends were traveling through Europe during the summer after high school, she had arranged for him to work on a Montana ranch. Any boyhood fantasies he had about the lure of the Old West were quickly replaced by the realities of 5:00 A.M. wake-up calls and painful blisters. He quickly decided that digging postholes and building fences was no way for him to spend a lifetime, and he eagerly returned home at summer's end.

"Look at my hands," he had complained when he came home. "These calluses are huge."

She had smiled. "I bet you dig the straightest postholes in all of Montana."

Doug looked down at his hands. *Those blisters and calluses—they were only the beginning of your plans for me, weren't they?*

chapter four

DARE TO BE
A PERSON,
NOT A POSITION

A few weeks later, Doug was hastily writing a note for his housekeeper when the telephone rang.

"Hello?"

"Mr. Roman, this is Jennifer. I hate to bother you," his secretary began apologetically.

"What's going on?"

"We need your approval on the budget changes so we can submit them to the bank."

"Can it wait until I get in? I'm running a little late and I still need to . . . well . . . what is it you said you need me to do?"

It was typical of Doug to pay only partial attention to her. "We need your approval on the budget changes. We're supposed to fax the changes by four o'clock. Will you be back in time?"

Doug didn't answer for a few seconds and then mumbled, "Well, I did say I'd be in later, didn't I?"

"Yes, Mr. Roman."

"Budget approvals, right?"

"Yes, Mr. Roman."

"I should be there by two o'clock. Please put everything on my desk. All right?"

"Yes, Mr. Roman."

Afterward, Doug thought about Jennifer. She had come to Mooseland directly from college, the daughter of a friend who needed a job. Doug never understood why Nan had hired Jennifer. Nevertheless, Nan had been confident in her choice. "You'll see," she had said, "Jennifer will be a part of the family."

Doug had countered, "Nan, this *isn't* a family. It's a business."

Nan had only smiled.

Jennifer did okay, he guessed, but she should just do her job and not worry so much about details. Doug decided that if Jennifer were a plant, she would most likely be a prickly nettle. Minimal contact with her often caused him irritation. Some garden he had to deal with! A prickly nettle and a stupid fern that shed on his Persian rug. Well, at least he had moved the fern from the dark pantry to the table under the entryway skylight. Elliott could not accuse him of reckless abandonment when it died.

Doug finished the instructions to his housekeeper, poured some water on the fern, which was looking a bit lackluster, and printed the e-mail from Anthony Ferrano.

Doug,
It was great to hear from you and I look forward to meeting you. I know it's short notice, but would your schedule accommodate a meeting at 9:00 Monday

morning? I leave Monday afternoon for the rest of
the week. Please let me know.
Regards,
Anthony Ferrano

Neither the business card he had received from Adoi nor Mr. Ferrano's e-mail message offered any hint as to why *he* would make room in *his* schedule for a stranger like Doug. For that matter, Doug was not sure why he was making room in his schedule for Mr. Ferrano. *What is the connection between Anthony Ferrano and Nan?*

Despite his misgivings, Doug approached the reception counter at Anthony Ferrano's building a few minutes before nine o'clock. *I don't have time to waste on this nonsense. I have a business to run. Instead, I'm chasing around after strangers, hoping to find my leadership legacy. This journey won't help to finalize the bank submission.*

"Good morning!" the receptionist greeted him warmly.

"Good morning," Doug replied in a strictly business tone, "Mr. Roman for Mr. Ferrano."

"I'll be happy to let his assistant know you're here. Please feel free to help yourself to something at the coffee and juice bar," she offered, motioning to a table with a variety of beverages and pastries a few feet away.

"Thank you," Doug said politely, but he discarded the idea of helping himself to any refreshment. *Mr. Ferrano's first picture of Doug Roman will not include a shirt covered with snack crumbs.* He turned to face one of the framed prints nearby and checked his appearance in the reflection in the glass.

Behind him, people who he presumed were employees strolled through the lobby, greeting others as they walked. Sometimes two or three stopped for a conversation that included so much laughter, he was sure the topic had more to do with personal escapades than work.

Doug shook his head, thinking that they behaved very much like Mooseland employees had when Nan had been around. He had pointed out more than once that workers wasting time in idle conversation were costing her money. Nan had only shrugged.

"Consider it an investment," she had said.

"An investment? In what?"

She hadn't answered. Now, as he watched these workers, he was reminded of their unfinished discussion.

Just then, a good-looking man with dark hair strode across the lobby in Doug's direction. Doug guessed him to be in his midfifties.

"Good morning, Tiphani," he bellowed. "How's your deck project coming along?"

"Good morning, Tony," she answered. "I think we'll finally finish it this weekend. You'll have to come over for the unveiling."

"Let us know when, and we'll be there!"

Must be some PR guy, Doug thought with disdain. *Doesn't he have any real work to do?*

The man continued toward Doug and stopped in front of him. "Hello. You must be Mr. Roman," he said, extending his hand to Doug. "I'm Tony Ferrano."

Caught off guard, Doug stammered, "Uh, good morning."

That's odd, Doug mused, trying to account for what he had just observed. *I thought his assistant would come down. Maybe his assistant is absent today. And all that friendly stuff with . . . what was her name? Tiphani?*

Meanwhile, Tony continued to pump Doug's hand. "Thank you for coming on short notice. I thought you might not want to wait until next week."

"It's a pleasure to meet you, Mr. Ferrano. Although I must confess, I'm not sure why I'm here."

Tony's smile broadened. "Please call me Tony. We try not to be formal around here." As they headed for the elevator, Tony continued. "Adoi is an amazing person. I'm always glad to meet a friend of hers. It's the least I can do."

Doug heard an echo of Nan in his words. Everyone who worked at Mooseland addressed her as "Nan." Doug preferred that his subordinates call him "Mr. Roman." He had always dismissed Nan's familiarity with her workers as a quirk in her nature. But Tony Ferrano did the same thing, and he was the president of a standout marketing firm.

Tony glanced at his watch. "My group is assembling for our weekly executive team meeting. These people are awesome, and I learn so much from them. We wrap up loose ends from the previous week, update ongoing projects and goals, and formulate short-term priorities for the upcoming week."

As they entered the elevator, Tony went on, "I e-mailed everyone and let them know you'd be joining us. Adoi no doubt told you that, as the special guest, you're scheduled to make a five-minute presentation about your company. We'll do that first."

What the heck is going on here? Doug looked expectantly at Tony, awaiting a further clue as to the meeting plan. *Adoi hadn't said anything about a presentation.*

Doug realized Tony was chuckling. "Just kidding, Doug," Tony exclaimed as he slapped Doug reassuringly on the shoulder. "I guess Adoi didn't tell you about my sense of humor."

Doug half smiled, again questioning his decision to meet with Tony Ferrano in the first place.

"Here we are," Tony said as the elevator doors opened. "And there's my crew," he added proudly, nodding toward the glass-walled conference room that adjoined the lobby. "Let's see if they've left any bagels for us, shall we?"

"Great," Doug answered as Tony led the way into the conference room.

"Hello, everyone!" Tony boomed.

Everything about the scene made Doug think more of an informal reception than a meeting of senior managers. Tony's eight executive team members were milling around a circular arrangement of upholstered sofas and armchairs, chatting and sipping beverages.

"Would you like some coffee or bottled water?" Tony asked Doug.

"Water would be great. Thank you."

"You got it." Tony turned and walked to the under-counter refrigerator. As Tony passed by his staff, each person greeted him in his or her own way, and Tony responded cordially.

"Thank you. But you didn't have to . . ." Doug protested when Tony returned with the water. "I would have—"

"Nonsense," Tony said. "You are our guest. Okay, everyone. Let's get started." Doug eased himself into one of the armchairs near where Tony was standing, then glanced at the faces around him. Two or three welcomed Doug to the meeting. It seemed to him they were actually eager to get started.

"Good morning!" Tony proclaimed. "I hope that you got a chance to read my e-mail about our guest, Doug Roman. He's a friend of mine and the future CEO of Mooseland Stoneware. Please welcome him when you have a chance.

"Last week, I announced that I would have the results of our customer survey for you today. Unfortunately, I overloaded Amy with preparations for the regional president's meeting. I've asked her to finish tabulating the data and distribute the summary in my absence. I apologize for the delay.

"I will be checking e-mail and voice mail while I'm away, so if there are any comments about the survey results or any other concerns, please leave me a message. If you need to reach me immediately, check with Amy.

"Well, Nick, let's roll and see where we'll begin today!"

All eyes in the room were trained on the coffee table in front of Nick as he rolled a pair of dice.

"Eight!" everyone who could see the dice said in unison.

"Who is lucky number eight this week?" Tony asked the group.

All heads turned as a young woman held up a piece of paper bearing the number eight.

"Carla!" Tony exclaimed. "What's happening in the world of Reichert Electronics?"

Doug was rattled by the contrast between the staff meetings he chaired at Mooseland and what he was seeing unfold here. When he walked into a meeting, Doug expected his subordinates to stay on their side of the table. It was obvious that Tony did not have the same expectation.

A confident female voice broke Doug's reverie. "Tony, we're suffering major heartburn with Reichert. We presented their decision makers with the entire layout on Friday expecting final approval—"

"And they want changes, Carla?" Tony smiled understandingly.

"Exactly. We've gone over and over this layout with them. We've responded to every one of their concerns. This was supposed to be the final presentation. We explained that if they continue to request revisions, we would have a problem with their deadline. The last thing we want is to push back the product launch."

Someone is to blame for this fire drill, and I would darn sure find out who, Doug thought. But Tony didn't react with anger. Instead, he extracted pertinent information by asking questions.

"I'm sure *that* news must have made them dance a jig," Tony cajoled.

"Pushing back the product launch is not an option, so they flexed. T. J. and Juanita and volunteers from Burke's team spent Saturday and Sunday mocking up the changes. We'll present the revisions tomorrow," she said with a shrug. "I'd like to let our weekend warriors leave at noon this Friday. They've gone 'above and beyond' on this one."

"I won't ask you or Burke how the greens treated you over the weekend. It sounds like you had your hands full," Tony said, smiling at Carla and nodding at Burke, an athletic-looking man who reminded Doug of a slightly younger, rough-cut version of Antonio Banderas.

"Thank your people for their efforts. Good call on the early departure on Friday. Keep me posted."

"Thanks, Tony."

"No problem. Okay, Burke, what's happening in production?"

Moving clockwise around the room, each attendee gave a summary of department happenings, project status reports, account updates, and budget results. Team members sometimes broke into dialogue that did not include Tony. At other times, Tony referred a question asked of him by one manager to another manager for comment.

Tony's approach bothered Doug.

What is wrong with an agenda listing items in order of importance? It's a meeting formula that works, right? True, my staff meetings aren't as lively as this one, but they get the job done. Maybe this is a show being staged for me.

The last to report was Nick. Looking serious, Nick straightened when Tony asked if he had anything he'd like to discuss. Doug had him pegged as Tony's CFO. *Okay, here we go. Tony's style may work for some of this staff, but now we're going to talk numbers.*

"Tony," Nick began, his voice soft compared to the others who had already spoken, "we've got a problem."

The postures of the assembled team members became more rigid and all random noise ceased. Everyone except Tony and Nick seemed to find something more important to look at outside the meeting circle.

Doug smiled to himself, relishing the thought of a little staff meeting excitement. *Aha! No more games for this group. Let's see how ol' Tony handles this one.*

"Nick, a situation is only a problem if we don't get it quickly into the hands of people qualified to handle it. Luckily, we are surrounded by experts. So, what's going on?"

Oh, come on! Nick is not going to go for that mumbo-jumbo team-building motivational jargon. Nick is my kind of man. He's a numbers guy.

Nick opened a portfolio and brought out a stack of spreadsheets.

"Ah," Tony said with a smile. "Looks like you brought ammunition."

"I hate to be the bearer of bad news, but we've been running heavy on overtime. It's time for a head-count discussion."

Nick glanced from Tony to the spreadsheets and then over to Burke. From the moment that Nick had first spoken up, Burke had clenched his jaws and tapped his pen repeatedly on his notepad.

"We are most overbudget in production," Nick said simply.

"Jeesh, Tony!" Burke exclaimed. "I am tired of having to justify production payroll." He waved his hand in Carla's direction. "You heard how Carla's problems impacted production. T. J., Juanita, Neil, Donna, Shivali, Jerry . . . they all knocked themselves out so the Reichert launch date would not be jeopardized. We're working overtime to complete what's in the pipeline. It doesn't make sense to cut payroll."

If Burke or any guy talked to me like that, I'd fire him on the spot.

"I see your point, Burke," Tony said. "Do you foresee that the spike in production is temporary, or do we need a longer-term solution? I can tell from our status reports that a ton of work is going out the door. I don't think it is in anyone's best interest to cut back where it appears we need more help."

Burke answered matter-of-factly. "I think we've got a busy six weeks ahead of us, and then the demands on our department should level off."

"But, Tony," Nick protested, "we must be cognizant of budget overages. We can't let this trend go unchecked."

"I don't know if this will help or not," Carla offered, "but we have two interns assigned to us for the summer. They've been helping with the ramp-up for Reichert. We could lend them temporarily to production. I'll need them back a few weeks before our presentation to Synergy Group."

"Is that workable for the short term?" Tony asked. Nick, Burke, and Carla all nodded their agreement.

"Good. Nick and Burke, please set a time with Amy for sometime next week, and we'll look at the long-term forecast. Maybe we need to make some midyear changes. We've taken on more new business than expected, so we might be running a little leaner than we intended."

Although he was still pumped up, Burke nodded. He knew it was a fair offer. "Thanks, Tony."

Tony looked around the room. "Anything else?"

Everyone seemed satisfied that this was a good place to end the meeting and began to disperse.

"Thank you, everyone. Good meeting, as always!" Tony said, rising from his chair. As the executive team members filed from the room, Doug noticed that Nick and Burke had begun speaking one-on-one in front of the refreshment counter. He made his way over to dispose of his water bottle, hoping to catch a bit of their conversation.

"I knew it was high." Burke was remarking to Nick as they turned and walked toward the lobby. "Thanks for bringing it out in the open so we could . . . "

Doug was stunned by this exchange. *Burke is not seriously thanking Nick, is he?*

Meanwhile, Tony was standing at the door. Doug noticed that he had a comment for each person that elicited a smile or nod from the recipient. When Burke and Nick reached him, Tony spoke quietly to them. When he was finished, both men grinned.

When Doug and Tony were alone in the room, Tony turned to Doug. "Well? What do you think?"

"That was some meeting," he said.

"Yes. They're an impressive group of people."

"Actually, I was talking about the way you handled the meeting," Doug said. "I wasn't sure how the issue with Nick and Burke was going to play out."

Tony nodded. "We place a high value on our people. Burke is no exception. He cares a lot for the people he supervises, as he should."

"Why did you start the meeting with a roll of the dice?"

"I don't remember when that started, but it was an attempt to let everyone know their department and their concerns are just as important as any other department or concern. Amy, my secretary, arranges for them to draw a number on the way in, Nick brings the dice, and away we go."

Tony and Doug walked toward Tony's office, situated on the opposite side of the lobby.

"It's a little unconventional, I suppose," Tony agreed. "Over the years, I've learned I can be a little less 'buttoned-up' and still accomplish some pretty fantastic things, but I'm not going to kid myself into thinking that I can do it alone. No one is an expert on everything.

"If I'm doing my job right, the leadership positions of the company will be staffed by people who are gifted in their chosen fields, they will have a clear understanding of our company's goals, and they will have access to the resources they need to dazzle us with their handiwork."

As they passed by his secretary's desk, Tony introduced Doug and Amy, thanked Amy for her help in getting everything ready for the meeting, and told her that Burke and Nick would be calling to set up an appointment.

In that moment, Doug reflected on the dialogue between Burke and Nick and Tony's calm response. *What is it about people like Tony and Nan? They can be in the middle of a heated debate, even the object of someone's anger, but they don't become heated or angry in turn. I don't think I ever saw Nan lose her cool with anyone at Mooseland.*

Tony ushered Doug into his office and pointed to a small photograph of himself as a younger man shaking hands with another young man.

"That's one of my most treasured mementos," Tony said nostalgically. "That's me on the left. And that's Adoi's father on the right. That picture was taken many years ago in front of his garden center. He was my first account after a little scrape that almost cost me my career."

Adoi's father?

"I was in my . . . what? midthirties," Tony reflected, "and quite the legend in my own mind. Marketing was my gift and I had landed some pretty big accounts." Tony grinned broadly at the memory. "And then reality."

"What happened?"

"I had been leading a team on a new marketing campaign for a major client. You can't imagine the hours we'd put into the campaign."

Doug shrugged. "Got to do what you got to do."

"That was my thinking," Tony said. "It was my career

and I was committed. The campaign was brilliant, Doug," Tony said, reliving the pride he had felt for his work.

"That was my team. I was their leader. And we were sitting on top of the world." His shoulders relaxed. "And then . . ."

Doug raised his eyebrows. "And then?"

"The company brought in someone new to supervise me and my team and to carry the project to the finish. Maybe they thought I was too young and did not have enough experience. I never really knew what prompted the decision. But I knew that I was angry. This guy was ruining everything. After a few weeks of listening to me bad-mouth him and every decision he made, the company made the only decision they could."

"What was that?"

"I was sent packing."

Doug was stunned.

"The new guy could have taught me a lot about the final phases of our project if I had let him. He offered constructive criticism; I defended my work. He was a great addition to the team. All I could muster was the feeling that my territory had been invaded by an enemy.

"I failed to recognize that the company had confidence in my abilities; otherwise, they would not have given me the project in the first place. It was a win-win for the company and me, but I missed my cue. I let an incredible opportunity slip through my fingers. That's when I met Adoi's father. First, he was a client, but he soon became a friend. We were both starting out; maybe that's why we hit it off. He certainly knew how to nurture his garden."

Oh, man! Here we go with the garden talk again. Does everyone live in a fantasy world but me?

"He taught me a lot about people and a lot about myself simply by the way he lived. He used to say, 'Tony, it's all about how you conduct yourself and treat people. It's about daring to be a person, not a position. Your title doesn't inspire or influence people, but your actions certainly do.

"Well, as I said, that was a long time ago, but I've spent a good many years bringing that person out from behind the nameplate."

Just as Doug was about to respond, Tony glanced at his watch. "Doug, I hate to cut our time short, but I'd better get to the airport."

This can't be the end of our meeting, Doug thought uneasily.

Resigned that it was time to leave, Doug looked one last time at the photograph before he extended his hand to Tony. "Thank you for seeing me so soon and making me feel welcome. Good luck with your travels."

"How about if you and I get together for lunch when I get back? I'd like to hear more about your plans for Mooseland."

"Well, sure, Tony. We'll set something up when things settle down a little bit." Doug's enthusiasm did not match Tony's, but Tony continued unfazed.

"And be sure to say hello to Adoi for me. It was my good fortune to have someone like her father in my life. Not everyone is so lucky."

Doug thought of Nan. He, too, was one of the lucky ones.

The Orchard Café

Checking his watch on the way out of Tony Ferrano's building, Doug decided to grab some lunch before heading back to the office.

TONY FERRANO

It's all about how you conduct yourself and treat people. It's about daring to be a person, not a position. Your title doesn't inspire or influence people, but your actions certainly do. I've spent a good many years bringing that person out from behind the nameplate.

What does he mean . . .
Dare to Be a Person . . . Not a Position?

- The meeting did not revolve around him

  Self-assured . . . but also humble?

- Not threatened by anyone

  Calm in a storm . . . not defensive

- Nobody would talk to me that way

  Keeps his ego in check

- What CEO admits mistakes?

  Takes responsibility for his actions

- Interesting team

  Seeks expertise and talent

- He served me, catered to them . . . huh?

  Respect for people at all levels?

- Does what he says he's going to do.

  Honest . . . go figure!

Now seated by the window at the Orchard Café, he reread the journal page he had just written. "I wonder why Adoi—"

"Hello, Doug."

Doug turned at the sound of her voice behind him. "Adoi." he said.

She nodded and smiled. "How are you, Doug?"

"I'm fine. It's a coincidence running into you. Do you have time to join me for lunch?"

"Well, I . . ."

"My treat," Doug added, hoping to convince her.

Adoi accepted and took the chair opposite him. "Who could say no to that deal? Besides, I'm wondering how the fern is doing in its new home."

"I'm happy to report that it's alive. But it doesn't seem as perky as it did at the garden center."

"Just remember what you noticed about its environment at the garden center, and you'll both be fine."

After they placed their orders, Adoi inquired about the coincidence Doug had mentioned.

"I just came from visiting Tony Ferrano," he said as their server brought glasses of iced tea.

"To tell you the truth, I'm not sure what I witnessed. He invited me to attend the weekly executive team meeting. The meeting had more give-and-take than what I'm used to. Tony seemed to sit back and observe a lot of the time. And he remained calm despite some obvious tension in the room.

"If it had been my meeting, I would have told everyone, 'Look, this is how it's going to be.' If you're in a leadership position, I think that's your job. People are counting on you to set the course and make decisions." Doug's voice trailed off as their server placed sandwiches and side salads in front of them.

Adoi picked up her fork and looked at Doug. "You know, Tony used to be wary of getting too close with any of his coworkers or clients."

"And then he met your father," Doug said slowly.

"Yes, and he learned the benefits of having the self-confidence and courage to seek people who possessed complementary talents. One of the truths that Tony learned is that he couldn't do his work alone. He figured out that the people around him needed to be collaborators, not just followers of the guy in charge."

"So, you're saying that Tony changed his attitude about other people."

"Perhaps he changed his attitude about himself first."

"Okay. He changed his attitude about himself and people, and it paid off. Maybe it was just a fluke." Doug was not convinced.

"A different approach worked for him, but who's to say that would be everyone's experience?" Doug enjoyed arguing his side of an issue, often failing to notice that his audience had no interest in debating him. Such was the case with Adoi as he continued. "You said it didn't happen overnight for Tony. How long does it take? How can I afford the time to go out and remake myself and still run a company? People are depending on me."

"Yes," Adoi said, "people are depending on you."

"Hi, Mr. Roman. Sorry to interrupt your lunch."

"That's okay, Brian." Doug was startled to see his production manager. "Adoi, this is Brian. Brian, Adoi." Everyone nodded as Doug handled the introductions.

Brian spoke with concern. "Mr. Roman, I apologize for

catching you during lunch. I looked over and saw you, and since I won't be back in the office until tomorrow, I thought I better let you know personally . . ."

"Gosh, Brian, what?"

"The main kiln is down. We've got the electricians working on the problem. I sent the production guys home. There wasn't anything for them to do."

"Brian, was that really the best course of action? We could have used those guys in shipping. Oh well, it's too late now."

"Sorry, Mr. Roman. It's just that—"

"No, let's leave it alone," Doug said with disappointment.

"I can call them back in, if you—"

"No. I'll see you tomorrow."

Sensing his dismissal, Brian said good-bye to Adoi and Doug and moved away from the table.

There was a brief pause as Adoi and Doug attempted to recollect where their previous conversation had been interrupted.

Adoi began. "I think we were discussing how Tony changed his attitude about himself, which, in turn, allowed him to view people around him differently. He transitioned from seeing his coworkers as duty-bound to carry out his instructions to capable colleagues with valuable experience and ideas. He learned to ask questions and appreciate the actions and decisions of his employees. Much like your aunt Nan."

Doug looked up and watched Brian leaving the café. "Yeah, I guess a question or two never hurts."

But at the mention of Nan's name, Doug stopped thinking about Brian and pictured Nan's letter instead. "Do

---

you think Nan intends for me to remake my life like Tony did? Is that the journey she had in mind? Am I supposed to find a friend like Tony found your father, develop a leadership legacy with my new friend in tow, and live out my days as the selfless, question-asking CEO of Moose-land?"

"It's probably tough to understand all that's happening right now," she said reassuringly. "You've still got a few months before the board meeting. Give it some time."

"There's no other choice, is there?" Doug replied. "I wonder what's next."

"Have you ever been to Eagle Junction?"

"It's been a long time, but yes. Nan took me there once when I was a kid. I don't remember much about our visit."

Adoi scribbled on a napkin and handed it to Doug.

"Historical Society, Monarch Street and Third, Esther Welling," Doug recited with a slight smile. "Another stop on the journey, Adoi?"

"When you have time," Adoi smiled back.

chapter five

DARE TO
CONNECT

My week is shaping up to be a bear, Doug thought as he parked his roadster at the community mailboxes Monday evening. His mind spun a review of the week's priorities. *Monthly financial reports are due at the bank by Friday, the presentation to Global Creations is scheduled for Wednesday, negotiations for the Hollis Brothers supplier agreement must be finalized, and—*

"Hey, Roman, how's it going?"

"Stein, what's up? What's new in the CPA world?"

Elliott pushed his glasses back up on his nose. "Not much." Elliott stuffed his mail into a tattered canvas pack. "I was thinking about heading over to The Cantina for a burrito. Want to join me?"

"You're on. Do you want me to drive? I wouldn't want us to get stranded if your, uh, vintage automobile breaks down."

Elliott laughed at the reference to his dilapidated '84 Volvo. "Oh, come on, let's live dangerously. It may not be the prettiest piece of machinery in the world, but it has a certain charm and it gets me where I'm going. I can't bring myself to get rid of it when it runs as well as it does."

A few minutes later, Elliott and Doug entered The Cantina as other sports fanatics settled in for the Monday night game.

"Are you making headway on the leadership legacy journey?"

"I'm not sure," Doug replied. "So far, we've got Adoi, a master gardener. You know all about her. Then I visited Tony, a CEO, and watched him preside over a senior staff meeting that had a few tense moments. He never lost his cool. I'm keeping a journal, but the notes don't seem to add up to much. You'll get a kick out of what I've got coming up."

Elliott's only reply was a questioning look.

"My next stop is Eagle Junction. Can you believe that? This is a leadership treasure hunt. Nan set the guidelines, and Adoi seems to be setting the itinerary." There was a big cheer as the visiting quarterback threw a pass right into the hands of a home-team defender.

"How's it doing so far?" Elliott asked as he dabbed futilely at a spot of salsa on his shirt.

"How's what doing so far?"

"The fern. How's the fern doing?"

"I took your advice and moved it to the hallway so it gets some light from the skylight. I've been pouring some water on it every morning, at least the mornings I remember. It seems to be shedding, and the leaves seem droopier than when I brought it home."

"It's not too late, Doug. Try misting it a couple of times a day. Better yet, if you have room near your shower, the warm moisture would be a real treat for it.

Leave it to Elliott to understand the needs of any other living thing.

"So, we know how the fern is doing. How are you holding up through all of this? Nan's death must have been a shock. The added news of not being named CEO must have been a double whammy."

Elliott's pleasant demeanor put Doug at ease. "Some days are better than others. I know Nan wanted the best for Mooseland and me. On the day Nan's will was read, Tommy pointed out that building a resume is not the same as building a leadership legacy. After I met Tony, I realized what makes an extraordinary leader has little to do with professional background. I'm really trying to discover what Nan sent me to find. Maybe it will all make sense one day."

Elliott requested more chips and salsa from their server. "The journal is a great idea. I read that writing in a journal ten minutes a day minimizes the risk of stress-related illness. I tell the kids at school to keep a journal. I can't think of anything more stressful than being a teen-ager."

"Elliott, you look young but not that young. What are you doing at school?"

"You're looking at a bona fide volunteer in the Winton High Career Mentors program."

"How long have you been doing that?"

"Several years now. I guess I started soon after we moved into our townhomes. Teenagers are in a tough spot. The prospect of making a curriculum choice that may, in turn, become a career choice is pretty daunting. The school's guidance counselors put together a program that matches students who are interested in a particular field with a career mentor who works in that field.

"Every couple of months they sponsor a 'Career Mentor Fair' and a bunch of us show up for an afternoon assembly. We each give a short presentation, and then we're available for one-on-one talks with kids who are interested in knowing more. These kids are great."

"Isn't it hard to communicate with teenagers?"

"I'll grant you that sometimes you have to listen a little harder than you do with your peers, but you catch on. A lot of times, the kids want to talk to someone who knows more about a particular field than their parents do. You know, 'What is it really like to be a superhero every April 15?' and all that."

Doug smiled at the thought of Elliott in a superhero costume with large CPA letters emblazoned on the front. "I'm impressed. But how do you find the time to be a career mentor? You work full-time-plus at Aberscher and Hutchins."

"I make the time. For the most part, these kids are bright and eager to do the right thing. It inspires me to spend a few hours here and there helping out. Hey, if you're not too busy tomorrow afternoon, stop in at the high school around one o'clock. I'll show you what I mean."

Doug was intrigued. "You know, I might see you there. It would be fun to see a superhero in action."

Winton High School

It had been years since Doug had set foot in his alma mater. He had taken off for college and never looked back. Keeping in touch with former high school classmates was never his thing. He was a future-oriented guy.

What was the benefit of feigning interest in relationships with people from his past with whom he had nothing in common?

"Hey, Doug, over here." Elliott's voice broke Doug's train of thought. "Is it just me, or do school hallways seem smaller than they did when we were kids?"

"Hi, Elliott. I'd have to say that the entire school seems smaller than when I went here."

"So, you're a Winton alum? Congratulations." Elliott was in his usual upbeat mood as he strode toward the auditorium. "The assembly starts in a few minutes, so let's go inside."

A few minutes later Doug was surrounded by noisy high schoolers. He nudged Elliott. "Did we look that young when we were their age?"

Elliott nodded. "Not only did we look that young, I'm guessing we sounded much younger than we thought we did. I think you'll see what I mean in a minute."

A guidance counselor brought the noisy bunch to order, welcomed the career mentors, and laid out the game plan for the afternoon. As Elliott had said the previous evening, career mentors would make a few comments, participate in a group question-and-answer session, and then be available at tables set up around the perimeter of the auditorium. Elliott called it a "career buffet."

". . . so please welcome our first guest, Elliott Stein."

Amid whoops, whistles, and applause, a smiling Elliott took the stage.

"Thank you, ladies and gentlemen. I'm joining you today from the fantastic world of public accounting!" Doug watched and listened as Elliott gave a quick sketch of his career. Elliott was a hit with the students and they listened intently to his remarks. When he was finished and asked for questions, several hands shot up. Elliott answered each question patiently.

"If I'm bad in algebra 'n' stuff, can I still be an accountant?"

"Like, if I became an accountant, like, would I have to, like, wear a suit every day?"

"If you're an accountant, do you make a lot of money? My parents are making me buy my own car."

"Can you get a job even if you don't get all As and Bs in college?"

Doug noticed that in each case Elliott repeated the question before answering it, making sure he understood the student's question. Once the student nodded, Elliott proceeded with his answer. He showed a vitality Doug was unprepared for: waving his arms, moving around the stage, and telling anecdotes from college and first-job days to illustrate his answers. Some of the questions amused Doug, but Elliott took each one seriously.

Near the close of his portion of the program, Elliott held up enlarged photos of graduates who had gone into accounting and highlighted their successes. He concluded with words of encouragement and an open invitation to visit Aberscher and Hutchins.

"That was great," Doug whispered as Elliott took his seat. "You made me want to become an accountant."

"Oh, no, my friend, not so fast. You already have a job."

"Well, only if the board lets me do it."

"You're going to nail it, Doug," Elliott reassured him.

Later, as they left the school, Doug again asked Elliott about his choice to become a career mentor.

"I have met some great young people, and if I can help someone accomplish something that they might not have accomplished otherwise, I get a rush of satisfaction. You probably know what I mean."

"Yeah," Doug replied, but honestly, he could not think of a time when he had had a similar experience.

"Your aunt's unexpected death must have hit everyone at Mooseland pretty hard," Elliott said. "Have you noticed any differences with your staff?"

Doug answered unsteadily. "We've got so much going on, I don't think they've had time to think about it."

Even to Doug's ears, characterizing Mooseland employees as people too busy with work to notice Nan was no longer there seemed wrong. It felt unjust to her memory and unfair to the employees, as well. Elliott let it pass.

"Mr. Stein?" a breathless young voice yelled from behind them. "Mr. Stein?" louder and closer this time.

Elliott turned to face a harried student. "Yes, what can I do for you?"

"Hi, I'm Luis and I was wondering if I could, uh, maybe, uh, come and visit you sometime. The thing is, I have a car and everything, but I work after school."

"Luis, I can appreciate a tough work schedule. Doesn't leave much time for much else, does it?"

"No, Mr. Stein. Not really."

"How about if we set up a time some evening or Saturday? Would one of those times work with your schedule?" Elliott dug in his jacket pocket and pulled out a business card. "Give me a call anytime, and we'll set something up."

As Elliott handed the card to Luis, Doug saw the now familiar fern emblem.

Well, what do you know about that? I should have known.

A few moments later, Luis and Elliott concluded their arrangements and Luis turned back to the school. Elliott picked up the conversation with Doug without missing a beat. "One of our VPs retired a year or so ago. He was the kind of person who dared to connect with people. He knew a little something about every employee—what part of the country they called home, their favorite sports team, things like that. Sometimes, he would sit down, talk for a few minutes, and really listen to what they had to say, making sure everyone had what was needed to get the job done. Most employees didn't see him on a daily basis, but everyone noticed a change in the atmosphere when he was no longer here."

Doug pondered Elliott's words for a bit. "I guess I'm not really sure how people are adjusting to Nan's absence."

"I remember your aunt mentioning how much she enjoyed the Mooseland family. Making genuine connections with people, getting to know them, listening to what they have to say. Maybe she thought that was a critical piece of her leadership legacy. You never know the future effects of such connections, whether you're there to witness them or not."

"Yeah," Doug said again. Until that moment he had never really considered the Mooseland employees to be *his* family, only Nan's. Looking back over his years at Mooseland, he had witnessed many occasions in which employees demonstrated their devotion to her. He recalled their tears at Nan's memorial service and realized that they had lost a beloved family member. He had not respected their loss.

"You know, Elliott, you're right about a couple of things."

"Like what?"

"The connection you're making with these kids will continue to pay dividends. And the connection Nan made with everyone at Mooseland continues, too. Mooseland is a pretty terrific family."

"Yeah, I think you're right."

"Oh, by the way, I moved the fern into the shower room last night. It already looks happier."

Later, at home, Doug checked his messages.

"Hi, Doug, I'm glad you and Elliott got a chance to talk. Give me a call at the garden center tomorrow and let me know how things are going."

Doug shook his head in wonder. "How does she do that?" he said to the inanimate recorder as it announced the date and time of Adoi's call.

ELLIOTT STEIN

He was the kind of person who dared to connect with people. He knew a little something about every employee— what part of the country they called home, their favorite sports team, things like that. Sometimes, he would sit down, talk for a few minutes, and really listen to what they had to say, making sure everyone had what was needed to get the job done.

Dare to Connect . . .
what does it look like?

- How does he understand their motivation?

  Asks questions?

- Nice how he picks up on other's perspectives

  Responds with empathy

- One-on-one talk . . . back and forth . . .

  Listens and repeats what is heard

- Wild how he broadcasts their successes

  Points out individual strengths

- Tiphani, Carla, Burke

  Remembers and uses names

- Draws people in

  Uses words and stories

chapter six

DARE TO DRIVE
THE DREAM

A few Saturdays later, Doug awoke to gray skies and drizzle. *I guess that takes care of my golf plans. Now what?*

His gaze settled on his journal and the napkin Adoi had given him. One shower, one shave, and two travel mugs of coffee later, Doug reached the outskirts of Eagle Junction, a charming mountain town nestled beside one of the largest natural lakes in the state.

Doug's knowledge of Eagle Junction was limited to what he had read in the newspaper. For decades, the town had sustained itself by catering to the streaming supply of tourists who wanted to "get away from it all" by visiting the undisturbed beauty of the national forest that abutted the lazy town's western border. Then a downturn in the economy dried up the flow of tourists and prompted a dramatic change.

After a period of heated public debates, the town had voted to allow casino gambling. A crop of modern buildings had sprung up, and an influx of new people and new jobs had revived the town's economy.

Doug's drive brought him past the newly constructed casinos and posh eateries. The new streets had names like "Lucky Lane," "Blackjack Avenue," and "Easy Street." The architects and developers had made an uninspired effort to blend the new buildings into the style of the original town. Sadly, the result was a line of demarcation, clearly signaling his passage from the new to the old.

Doug kept driving until he came to a small cobblestone traffic circle in the center of the town's older district. Rustic wooden signs directed drivers to free public parking, visitor information, the public library, and the town hall.

The storefronts facing the main street appeared to be quaint homes that had been renovated to provide commercial space on the first floor and efficiency living quarters on the upper floors. Doug sensed that in Eagle Junction, walking was the best way to get from point A to point B, so he left his car at the free public parking lot beyond the roundabout.

The Historical Society at Monarch Street and Third turned out to be a five-minute walk away. The building was a small home with white clapboard siding and green shutters. A large antique wood door with oval bevel-edged glass stated "Eagle Junction Historical Society" in gold and black lettering in a half arc, reminiscent of the lettering Doug had seen on banks in old Western movies. The lower curve of the glass was bordered with delicate ferns.

Once inside, Doug observed that the front of the house had been converted into one long, open room. Shelves and wood-framed glass display cases were all around, housing books, photographs, maps, legal documents, and memorabilia from a bygone era.

"Welcome, sir," an enthusiastic voice trumpeted from the back of the room. "How may the Eagle Junction Historical Society assist you today? My name is Esther Welling, and I am at your service."

"Mrs. Welling—" Doug began his reply to the petite, elderly woman walking toward him.

"First," the lively woman interrupted, waving him off with one of her arthritic hands, "if we're going to be friends, you'll have to stop calling me Mrs. Welling. That was my mother-in-law, God rest her lovely soul. I was never partial to 'Mrs. This' and 'Mr. That.' So, how about if you call me Esther? Now, how I may help you?"

"Okay, uh, Esther. My name is Doug Roman. Adoi gave me your name."

"Adoi!" she exclaimed, clasping her hands over her heart and smiling broadly at the sound of Adoi's name. "Such a wonderful child. How is she?"

"She's fine, ma'am," Doug smiled politely.

"I'm not as mobile as I once was, but my friend Clara has family near Adoi's lovely Truth Seekers Garden Center, so we visit a few times a year. It's a rejuvenating place, isn't it?"

Doug responded with more tact than sincerity. "Yes, it's very nice."

"So, can I help you find something? Do you have ancestors that passed through Eagle Junction?"

"I have a feeling that finding long-lost ancestors would be child's play compared to my current project. You might say that Adoi has sent me on a scavenger hunt, except that I don't know what I'm looking for and I'm not sure what to do with it if and when I find it. Sounds crazy, doesn't it?"

"Well," she said laughing, "sometimes you have to work a little to accomplish something worthwhile."

Before Doug could respond, the door opened and in walked a woman he thought to be about Esther's age.

"Clara, you're early," Esther exclaimed. "I can't leave my post whenever the mood strikes."

"Oh, Esther, you know you run this town. Besides, we have work to do," Clara chided Esther good-naturedly. "Who is your handsome friend?"

"Clara, this is Doug, and don't even think of flirting with him. I saw him first. He's a friend of Adoi's."

Doug smiled self-consciously as the women he figured to be at least forty years his senior shamelessly vied for his attention.

"You're a friend of Adoi's!" Just like Esther, Clara seemed overjoyed at the sound of Adoi's name. "Adoi has been a great friend to my family. And I love visiting the garden center whenever I can. My daughter and her family live only a few miles from there. Welcome to Eagle Junction!" Clara beamed proudly. "The least we can do, Esther, is to give Doug a tour of our fine town while he's here."

"Really, I couldn't impose," Doug protested.

"Tell you what, Doug. Clara and I had planned to treat ourselves to lunch at Finney's while we discuss a little project we're working on. How about if we all go for a short walk," Esther suggested, "and then you can join us for lunch."

"That is a superb idea, Esther," Clara chimed in. "We can show him our wall."

"Oh, yes. The 'wall' that Clara is referring to is our lovely mosaic."

"Well, it will be lovely if we ever finish it." Clara's voice betrayed a hint of frustration.

"Now, Clara, we'll find a way to finish it." Esther was having no part of Clara's concern. "We've gotten this far, haven't we?"

"I suppose you're right. But it's hard to be positive when our project is on the brink of failure."

"We won't give up now. There's an answer out there waiting for us to find it. Let's show Doug the wall. Maybe he'll have an idea or two."

To Doug, the conversation between these two women was a bit haunting. Nan, too, had remained calm in the face of problems and used encouraging words similar to Esther's countless times during his life. He, on the other hand, was a realist. *It's tough, but sometimes situations don't turn out the way you'd like them to. I was reminded of that in Tommy McCann's office a couple months ago.*

Esther locked up the building and moments later, Doug found himself between two attentive tour guides, strolling arm in arm down Monarch Street. They knew the history of each building they passed, and they delighted in relating obscure tidbits about the families who had occupied them over the last century and a half. *What "brink of failure" could these two possibly be facing?*

They reached the town hall and adjoining park a few minutes later. "This park has played host to recitals, concerts, graduations, fund-raising carnivals, Fourth of July celebrations, and family reunions for as long as I can remember," Esther remarked nostalgically. "It's a place where our town comes together as a family."

Clara picked up the story. "Esther and I did not support our town's decision to embrace casinos and gambling as a means to preserve our town's future. We lamented our loss, but then it occurred to us. "Maybe preservation of the town's *future* was out of our hands, but preservation of the town's past was not."

"We dreamed of a permanent Eagle Junction family 'scrapbook,' one that townspeople could look at anytime," Esther continued the tale. "Something that would remind our current residents and future generations of the town's rich history and the men and women who have lived here since its founding in the mid-1800s."

"So, you put together a scrapbook?" Doug asked, thinking that any unforeseen circumstance related to an unfinished scrapbook scarcely qualified as the "brink of failure" in his world.

"Not exactly," Clara sighed. "A few years ago, we were walking through this park and we both happened to look at the barren wall of the town hall that borders the park."

As if on cue, both women turned and faced the wall behind them.

Doug followed their example and turned.

The left side of the drab taupe-gray town hall had been partially transformed into a mosaic mural depicting the town as it had appeared in its early days.

Esther squeezed Doug's arm and sighed loudly. "Magnificent . . . don't you think?" she said with delight.

"As you can see, it is a work in progress." Clara said. "Work was halted last week when our funding was unexpectedly terminated. There's more," Clara promised as she and Esther began walking toward the mosaic for a closer inspection.

Doug was surprised to see that the big image that was visible from a distance was composed of thousands of small tiles, each of which contained an artistic rendering of an Eagle Junction historical fact or memento. The detail was incredible.

"This is your 'scrapbook'?" Doug asked incredulously. "I've never seen anything like it. How does one even begin a project like this?"

"What you see took several years of work and involved a lot of people," Esther said with energetic sincerity. "We pored through archived records, photographs, and newspapers; made an exhaustive search for living descendants of the town's early settlers; and met with neighboring historical societies and museum curators, all in an effort to gather as much information as we could about our town's history."

"It was tedious work," Clara said, "but we worked together and it seemed our dream would become a reality until we got a letter from our funding source. Money for our project must be approved annually. Due to budget constraints, our proposal was not renewed for the upcoming year."

"Oh my!" exclaimed Esther. "I remember getting the call from Ms. Chen. She felt so bad. I said, 'Don't you worry . . . it's going to take more than an old stack of dollars to stop this train.'" She smiled at Doug. "We've just come too far . . . and honestly, we're having too much fun to give up!"

Doug felt a strange sense of nostalgia about Esther's determined drive.

So now what?" Doug asked. "It's going to cost a small fortune."

"The price tag of our dream has always been a challenge," said Clara, "but then again, it keeps us looking for new ideas . . . the 'what if's.' At our age, that's quite an adventure."

"We're like pioneer women in unmapped territory," Esther explained. "But, with the help of our wizard-friend, Jason, we got this far. Maybe he can work his magic again. Jason is pretty good with that computer of his. He conceptualized the project. Then he and his friends organized a mail campaign. We sent a letter describing our project to all Eagle Junction residents and their relatives, as well as all out-of-town descendants we could contact. We asked them to search scrapbooks, family Bibles, and storage trunks for Eagle Junction hidden treasure."

Clara's eyes twinkled as she explained further. "Then we suggested 'donating' tiles in honor of living loved ones and in memory of those who had passed on. Our vision was that each tile would contain an inscription noting who had donated the tile and who was being honored or remembered. Beyond its aesthetic appeal, one of the beautiful aspects of our wall would be its perpetual availability."

"Clara and I were in a bit of a pickle. Donations for tiles started flowing in and we had no idea how we were going to construct a mosaic wall!" Esther was amused at the memory of the project's early days. "But we could picture it, and we wanted to make it happen, so we plowed on."

Doug kept staring at the wall as he listened to their unbelievable tale.

"Jason was persistent in his research of possible funding sources to underwrite the construction costs. He discovered the Historical Preservation Council. He and his friends have been a godsend to us in so many ways."

"He's precious, all right," Clara concurred. "Shall we adjourn to lunch?"

The short walk to Finney's gave Esther and Clara another opportunity to entertain Doug with little-known facts about Eagle Junction.

"Here we are!" Esther announced as she pushed through the vintage saloon-style doors at the entrance to Finney's. "Jason, did you save us some pie?" she called to the grinning twenty-something, ponytailed man behind the counter.

"Absolutely! I know not to get between you two and homemade pie," Jason called back. Laughter rippled around the room.

As Doug seated himself at the bar, which looked like it had been borrowed from a John Wayne movie set, Jason extended his hand and introduced himself.

"I'm Jason Lightfoot, and I'm proud to call those women my friends." Jason nodded toward Esther and Clara, who had gone to say hello to other diners.

"I'm Doug," Doug said, shaking Jason's hand. "I haven't known Esther and Clara for very long, but I admire your choice of friends. They've been showing me all around town."

"I'll have to agree with you on that. They have endless energy. We've suffered a little setback on our project, but with those two around, it won't be for long."

"They say you are a wizard, but they didn't tell me how you became involved."

"Yeah, we look like pretty mismatched business partners, don't we?" Jason laughed. "But, in fact, we make a great team. I'm an art history major with a minor in graphic design, and I love the mountains. There aren't many jobs for art history majors who want to go skiing six months out of the year. I'm a pretty decent cook, and Finney's offered flexible hours, so I signed on.

"One day, Esther asked me if I would be willing to work on the mosaic project with them. I'm not sure what I want to do when I grow up, and this seemed like something I could get excited about." After a short pause, Jason added, "Who in their right mind could refuse them? Once they get something in their heads, they don't take no for an answer. Know what I mean?"

"I think I'm getting there," Doug said, nodding.

"I never imagined two fine ladies like Clara and Esther could inspire a guy like me. You get caught up in their passion and persistence. It's like *anything* is possible if you just dare to drive the dream. I'm telling you, I have no doubt that they'll see it through to the end, and I for one want to be around when it happens. This commitment they have, it's kind of contagious. Man, what a legacy."

Did Jason just say legacy? Doug looked up at Jason's choice of words just as Esther and Clara were making their way back to the counter.

"Lunch today, or are you skipping ahead to dessert?" he asked the group.

After some discussion, everyone settled on the lunch special, which included a sandwich, homemade soup, and, of course, a slice of Finney's "infamous" lemon meringue pie. Between bites, Esther, Clara, and Jason discussed their predicament.

"Abandoning the project is not an option," Esther told the others, "so that means we have to secure alternative funding. Don't be shy. Any ideas?"

"What if we send a newsletter to everyone in our database?" Jason was already writing the copy and mocking up the layout in his mind.

"You may be on to something," Esther said. "We could

include a picture of the wall and some anecdotes we've received from contributors."

"Can we afford a mailing like this?" Clara asked.

"Somehow we have to send an SOS. Can we afford not to do it?" Esther replied.

Clara and Jason nodded their agreement with Esther's point.

"We'll cut costs if we send the newsletter electronically to everyone who gave us their e-mail address," Jason offered. "I'll bet we can contact at least half of our pool that way."

Doug listened as the ad hoc task force kicked around some ideas. The discussion continued until they had formulated a plan and divvied up assignments.

After lunch, Esther said she had to get back to the historical society, Clara had a hair appointment, and Doug figured he'd better be heading home. Esther and Clara charged Doug with passing along their greetings to Adoi. The trio exchanged farewell pleasantries and went their separate ways.

Leaving town, Doug realized he was still a bit keyed up from spending time with Clara and Esther. As he passed from picturesque to glitz, he thought about Clara and Esther's dedication. The mosaic wall, once a vague "scrapbook" dream, might someday serve as a monument to Eagle Junction's past and the power of persistence.

As he reached the outskirts of town, the sound of Esther's voice echoed in his mind, "Sometimes you have to work a little to accomplish something worthwhile."

Doug was considering his promise to pass along Esther and Clara's greeting to Adoi when his cell phone rang.

"Hello?"

"Hello, Doug. This is Adoi."

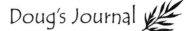

ESTHER AND CLARA

*You get caught up in their passion and persistence. It's like
anything is possible if you just dare to drive the dream.
I'm telling you, I have no doubt that they'll see it through
to the end, and I for one want to be around when it happens.
This commitment they have, it's kind of contagious.*

What do they do
to Drive the Dream?

- The wall, the wall, at   *Relentlessly committed*
  all costs, the wall   *to their dream*

- They like to ask   *Welcome risk or change*
  "what if "

- So many obstacles . . .   *Remain optimistic*
  the unforeseen   *always*

- "The details" . . .   *Figure out ways to*
  what, why, and how   *execute*

- Everyone is smiling . . .   *Genuinely have fun . . .*
  how do they do that?   *infectious*

chapter seven

THE FERN
IS REVIVED

"Hey, buddy, are you ready for another great day at Mooseland?" Doug pointed the mister at the lush fern and squeezed a few sprays onto the vibrant deep green fronds, while checking the moisture content of the soil with his other hand. He heard a noise outside his ofice and called out, "Jennifer? Is that you so early?"

"Yes, Mr. Roman," Jennifer appeared at the door in seconds. "I know it's short notice, but my grandmother is coming to town and I'd like to leave a little early this afternoon."

Doug hesitated. "That will be, um, fine. What's on my schedule today?"

"Your weekly meeting with Brian is at nine, the Global Creations team meeting is scheduled in the main conference room at ten, the Mighty Moose luncheon is at noon, and, of course, the board meeting is at four."

Jennifer's delivery of the last item sounded ominous.

Indeed, "the board meeting" needed no further explanation to anyone at Mooseland. Since the reading of Nan's will six months ago, the subjects of "who would become the next CEO" and "the board meeting" that would decide Doug's future had been discussed in detail.

Everyone knew that the day of "the board meeting" had arrived.

"Oh, I forgot that was today," Doug said facetiously. "Well, I suppose whatever is going to happen is going to happen." He took a deep breath and looked out the window at nothing in particular. "It's fine for you to leave early. So, where's your grandmother from?"

"Eagle Junction. She's driving down with her friend, Esther, and I worry about them driving back after dark."

"Her friend's name is Esther?"

"Yes, Esther," Jennifer repeated, looking up at him.

"Is your grandmother named Clara?" Doug smiled as Jennifer's head nodded.

"How did you know that?"

"It's a small world. I met your grandmother and Esther a few months ago. How is it going with the mosaic wall? When I visited them, they had lost their funding, but they were determined to press on."

"This is unbelievable." Jennifer was stunned that Doug had met her grandmother and Esther. "The wall is beautiful, or it will be. Grandma told me that one of the descendants of the first Eagle Junction mayor responded to an e-mail campaign and offered to underwrite the remaining design and construction costs."

"Wow! They did it!" Doug laughed, glad that the two women had succeeded. "It was a pleasure to meet your grandmother and her friend. Please say hello for me."

"Of course," Jennifer replied.

"Since I have some time before Brian arrives, I'm going to take another look at my notes for the board meeting," Doug said as he lifted his journal and a presentation folder from his briefcase. "Please hold my calls."

"Okay. I have one item. Tony Ferrano called and said, 'Good luck.' He also wondered about lunch next week. He just returned from a leadership conference and he wants to tell you about it. Should I schedule it?"

"Go ahead and set it up for early next week. Depending on the board's decision, I may have loads of time next week." Doug grinned, partly because he was apprehensive about the board meeting and partly at the thought of Tony. "He is something. We relax and laugh a little, and he's usually pretty inspirational."

"Judging from my conversations with him, Tony always seems ultra-energized," Jennifer commented as she wrote herself a note.

I, on the other hand, seem to fade when the situation calls for inspiring people.

Doug looked at a small photograph of Nan congratulating last year's recipient of the Mighty Moose Employee of the Year award. *Nan's style was more reserved than Tony's, but she also knew how to inspire people. Hopefully, I'll get better at it. I'm trying, Nan. I'm trying.* Doug was lost in thought for a few seconds more before something clicked in his mind. "Jennifer, when Nan hired you, she told me you were the daughter of a friend. Was Nan acquainted with your mother?"

"Yes and no. Both Nan and my mother were friends of a woman named Adoi. She runs the Truth Seekers Garden Center."

"I also met Adoi a few months ago. It is a small world, isn't it?"

"Yes. Adoi heard from my mother that I was graduating from college and looking for a job. She mentioned it to Nan, and, well, here I am."

"For Mooseland's sake I'm glad you needed a job. I mean, I'm glad you agreed to work here. It wouldn't be the same without you, so, uh, thanks."

"You're welcome," Jennifer answered sincerely.

"Well, back to work. Please let me know when Brian arrives, assuming he hasn't taken a sick day to recuperate from the miserable performance of the Warriors last night. He keeps telling me it's a 'rebuilding' year," Doug chuckled.

"Okay, Mr. Roman," Jennifer replied, smiling at the reference to Brian's beloved baseball team, which had floundered for years. "Mr. Roman?"

"Yes?"

"I miss Nan, but I'm glad I've had the chance to work with you, too. You're getting to have more in common with Nan in how you handle people and situations. Anyway, good luck today."

"Thanks, Jennifer," Doug said, buoyed by the unexpected comparison to Nan. "I'm going to give it my best shot." *Okay, Nan. Comparing Jennifer to a prickly nettle was off the mark. It's great to have her in the Mooseland family, like you knew it would be.*

Doug's morning proceeded as planned, and he finished his appointments in time to arrive a few minutes early for the Mighty Moose luncheon in the garden event center. He was greeting employees when a familiar face appeared.

"Adoi, what a nice surprise." *How does she always know where to find me?*

"Hi, Doug. I was in the neighborhood, so I thought I'd stop in."

"I'm glad you did," he said with a smile. "Do you have plans for lunch? There's always room for one more at the Mighty Moose luncheon."

"Mighty Moose?"

"The Mighty Moose idea was Nan's. We honor departments and individuals who have given extraordinary effort and achieved high goals during the past year. Nan felt strongly that Mooseland could only be as strong as its employees, and she urged employees to envision a mighty Mooseland. Over the years, the Mighty Moose awards were born. The top award is Mighty Moose Employee of the Year. The recipient's identity is kept secret until the moment the award is presented."

"She knew how to nurture the Mooseland family, didn't she?"

"I used to view this as another silly excuse for employees to get a free meal on the company and take unnecessary time off from work."

"And now?"

"Well, I suppose it gives me a chance to let everyone know how important their leadership and participation are for Mooseland's future. I've been working on my remarks, so I hope I get across what I'm trying to say. I'm still rusty when it comes to public speaking."

"I think Nan would be pleased with the choice of this year's emcee. And I think Brian will be pleased with the recognition of Mighty Moose Employee of the Year. I gather that over the past few months you gained a new understanding of Brian."

"Yes, I think he will be too. But, how do you know . . . ?"

She just smiled.

The Board Meeting

The special meeting of the Mooseland Stoneware Board of Directors took place in the main conference room and began promptly at 4:00 P.M. The board members took seats on one side of the rectangular table, and Doug and Tommy took seats on the other.

The acting chairman spoke first. "I welcome all who have gathered for this special meeting of the Mooseland Stoneware Board of Directors.

"Mr. Roman," the acting chairman looked squarely at Doug, "we will begin with your comments. You are free to address this board in whatever manner and for whatever time frame you choose. Following your remarks, the board will have the opportunity to question you.

"At the conclusion of the question-and-answer period, the board may render a decision or proceed with a closed-door session. For the record, according to Ms. Nanette Roman's request, this board must confirm the next CEO and chairman of Mooseland Stoneware unanimously. Please begin when you are ready, Mr. Roman."

With that, all eyes shifted expectantly to Doug.

Wanting the board to recognize his new understanding of leadership legacy and his suitability to be the next CEO, he began to tell of his journey over the last six months—the stops he made along the way and the transformations that had taken place.

First, he described his visits with Tony Ferrano, who taught him to *Dare to Be a Person, Not a Position*. "Tony understands his strengths and limitations and how to be self-assured without being arrogant. He readily admits his mistakes and takes responsibility for his actions. He recognizes that he cannot be an expert in all areas, so he purposely surrounds himself with experts to balance his team."

Then he spoke about his neighbor and unexpected mentor, Elliott, who *Dares to Connect with People*. "Elliott has a gift for empathizing with people and seeing their strengths, no matter the circumstance, his or theirs."

Finally, he told about his adventure in Eagle Junction, where he met the dynamic duo, Clara and Esther, two excellent examples of leaders who *Dare to Drive the Dream* with their contagious passion for the pursuit of positive results. "When I met Esther and Clara, I came face-to-face with indomitable persistence and tireless energy working together to achieve a lofty goal."

Doug paused, took a deep breath, and continued.

"I believe my work to date at Mooseland speaks for itself regarding my business acumen. You all have copies of my resume, and I will be happy to answer any specific inquiries you may have regarding current financials and future business goals."

Glancing briefly at Tommy he said, "However, a wise man once told me that building a resume differs from building a leadership legacy. The purpose of our meeting is to focus on the character of Mooseland's next leader and CEO and the environment that he or she will cultivate for Mooseland's greatest asset, its people. My experiences of the last six months have compelled me to look closely at Mooseland's family. Although I cannot take credit for the extraordinary people with whom I have the honor to work, I am proud of what I see. Mooseland is a place where complementary skills, styles, and personalities blend and reinforce each other. It is a place where people are glad to come for a good part of their day. We all have Aunt Nan to thank for that. It is her legacy.

"The truth about my own journey is that I don't fully know what my leadership legacy is. I only know what it *can't* be. I believe I have made great strides to incorporate the three leadership imperatives I observed during my journey. But I cannot honestly say that my progress is enough and that I am living an exemplary leadership legacy.

"I think I have a better sense of my strengths and weaknesses. I strive to take responsibility for my actions and to conduct myself with integrity. But do I consistently *Dare to Be a Person, Not a Position?* Maybe not yet.

"I honestly believe I have become more aware of the people with whom I work; I attempt to see situations and issues from their perspective and understand how they approach their work. I look forward to our conversations and to their input. But truthfully, I've got a long way to go before I can say I fully *Dare to Connect with People.*

"Finally, I must say I feel an inspiration that I haven't felt before. My journey has allowed me to look through the passionate eyes of others, and it somehow has brought me back to the dream that was Nan's: To Mooseland—its outstanding history and hopefully its bright future. I'd like to be a part of generating excitement for Mooseland's possibilities. I'm looking at commitment and risks in a whole new way these days. Will I be able to inspire others as I *Dare to Drive the Dream?* That will have to be my employees' call.

"For the first time in my life, I am acutely aware that my personal journey to a leadership legacy has only begun. The inscription written by Nan in the front of my journal states, 'As your journey reveals the truth, write it. As the truth reveals your legacy, live it.'"

"Well, the truth is, while I want the opportunity to try, I may not be ready to serve Mooseland as its CEO. Therefore, I respectfully suggest that you table the vote regarding my confirmation for one year so that I may continue the journey Aunt Nan planned for me. Thank you."

The room was silent for several moments.

Finally, the acting chairman spoke. "We appreciate your comments and recommendation. I'm sure you realize that we take our responsibility seriously to render a decision consistent with Nan's request.

"We have the difficult assignment to weigh all information available to us and to pass a resolution that will monumentally impact the future of Mooseland and its people. We need to give due consideration to your experiences over the past six months, as well as your suggestion to delay our decision for another year.

"However, we would be remiss if we failed to acknowledge the recharged atmosphere at Mooseland, certainly a difficult challenge in the wake of Nan's death. It seems that instead of dwelling on the past, many employees are excited about the future. You might like to know that many employees feel they have been able to pull together under your leadership and have continued to envision great possibilities for our company."

As he spoke, he opened a folder containing what appeared to be a short stack of mismatched pieces of paper clipped together.

"That is not just our opinion. Over the past several weeks, the board has received a steady stream of unsolicited letters from Mooseland employees at all levels.

Without exception, they unanimously urge the board to . . . how did one person put it?" he said, shuffling through the stack, "Oh yes, here it is. The board would be certifiably nuts to let this leader get away. Please do whatever it takes to keep Doug leading the Mooseland team.'"

Doug glanced again toward Tommy, who offered a small nod and friendly grin.

"Therefore, based on this board's observations of your demonstrated desire and capacity to *Dare to Be a Person, Not a Position; Dare to Connect with People;* and *Dare to Drive the Dream* and the Mooseland family's overwhelming recommendation, the board unanimously agrees that Doug Roman shall be confirmed as CEO of Mooseland Stoneware, effective immediately."

Doug sat motionless, not yet ready to respond.

"Doug, the board urges you to continue your journey. This is the leadership legacy that Nan left for each one of us. We should all continue to develop and flourish. I hope you will accept this appointment with our congratulations and the knowledge that it is our unqualified conclusion that there is no one better suited to lead Mooseland."

Nan's Office

"Are you as shocked as I am?" Doug asked Tommy as they made their way down the hall outside the conference room.

"No, not entirely," Tommy replied. After a pause, he continued, "I hope I'm not being presumptuous, but I believe that if Nan had been able to hear you today, it would have been her proudest moment." Tommy held out his hand. "May I say, it is an honor and pleasure to know you."

Doug returned the handshake, thanking Tommy and promising to call him. After Tommy left, Doug had the odd feeling that he didn't know what to do next.

Oh, Nan. I wish—Doug's thoughts were interrupted by the telephone ringing in Nan's former office.

Picking it up on the third ring, he said, "Hello?"

"Doug, how did the meeting go?" Adoi inquired.

"Adoi, how did you know I would be here? I didn't even know I was going to be here. In fact, I was just in the hallway . . ." Doug's mind could not make sense of Adoi's mystical radar or whatever it was she used to track him.

"I have something for you."

"Another plant, Adoi? Have I not proven myself already with the fern?" he said lightheartedly.

"First tell me about the meeting," Adoi directed.

Doug then relayed all that he could remember about the remarkable events that had unfolded moments before.

There was complete silence at the other end of the line.

"Adoi? Are you still there?"

"You did it." Adoi's words came slowly. "In six months, you succeeded in grasping what Nan so desperately wanted you to learn. Congratulations."

"I hope I can live up to their expectations—Nan, the board, my coworkers."

As Doug spoke, he still felt a bit of disbelief.

"And your own," said Adoi. "Doug, open the bottom right drawer of Nan's desk."

"The desk is locked," Doug explained. "I couldn't open it if I wanted to. Besides, we cleaned out the desk after Nan died."

"Open the bottom right drawer," Adoi repeated.

Doug did as Adoi asked and was surprised to feel the drawer open and to see a hinged wooden box inside. He lifted the box from the drawer and set it on the middle of the desk. An ornate carving of a fern decorated the top of the box, and a simple brass hook and eye served as the closure.

"Nan asked me to deliver this box to you." Adoi talked as if she were standing next to him and could see everything he was doing.

Inside were two items. First was Nan's journal, detailing her hopes and thoughts and wishes pertaining to Mooseland Stoneware since its founding, along with personal principles she had set for herself. Doug was not surprised that her notes coincided with his experiences over the past six months.

The other item was a small box. Doug lifted the cover and was astonished to see business cards—white business cards with an embossed fern in the upper right corner and these words centered on the card: "Doug Roman, Chairman and CEO, Mooseland Stoneware."

"I owe so much to you, Adoi. What now?" Doug asked.

But she was no longer there.

MY PRINCIPLES
by Nannette Mae Roman

*The journey to Living Your Leadership Legacy
begins with what you believe.*

I BELIEVE YOU MUST DARE TO
BE A PERSON, NOT A POSITION

- Be self-assured but also humble.
- Be calm in a storm, not defensive.
- Keep your ego in check; gain commitment rather than compliance.
- Readily admit your mistakes and take responsibility for your actions.
- Seek expertise and surround yourself with talent.
- Demonstrate respect for people at all levels.
- Do what you say you are going to do.
- Be honest.

I BELIEVE YOU MUST
DARE TO CONNECT WITH PEOPLE

- Ask questions to explore the motivations of others.
- Respond to the perspectives of others with empathy.
- Make a point to talk one-on-one with people.
- Listen intently, and repeat back what you heard.
- Point out people's individual strengths to them.
- Remember and consistently use people's names.
- Broadcast the successes of others.
- Use words and stories to draw people in.

I BELIEVE YOU MUST DARE TO
DRIVE THE DREAM

- Remain relentlessly committed to a dream.
- Help people to see the outcome of the dream in years to come.
- Keep asking "what if" before a plan is finalized.
- Welcome risk or change if it serves the dream.
- Figure out ways to narrow the gap between what is and what is desired.
- Remain optimistic regardless of unforeseen obstacles or naysayers.
- Tackle the details of "what," "why," "where," and "how."
- Genuinely have fun.

ACKNOWLEDGMENTS

We'd like to acknowledge several important people in our lives.

Marta wishes to thank her family and friends who have traveled this journey with her and taught her many valuable lessons about life and love. Special thanks go to Tim, the center of her life and her reason. "My legacy is safe in your heart. Grow old with me; the best is yet to come."

Julie thanks her parents and siblings, who are her models for living well and whose legacy she's proud to share. She wishes to recognize Ben and Noah, who remind her daily what a privilege it is to live and learn. She's especially grateful to her best friend and husband, Steven, her anchor and her sails.

Sarah would like to thank her daughter, who teaches her a new lesson in leadership each day. She also wishes to acknowledge the Blanchards, who have provided a wonderful "laboratory" for learning and a positive, supportive environment to work in. Special thanks go to her husband, Rob, for providing inspiration and patience throughout this process.

Finally, thank you Kevin Karaffa and Linda Moore for truly living *Your Leadership Legacy*.

ABOUT THE AUTHORS

Marta Brooks has been a highly respected and experienced management consultant, as well as a powerful trainer and motivational speaker, for the past fifteen years. She developed her business acumen by traversing the worlds of corporate management and personal entrepreneurship. She uses her hands-on business expertise to inspire leadership effectiveness and promote individual accountability for desired results.

Marta's signature speaking topic is "Your Leadership Legacy: Making a Positive Difference in People's Lives."

Marta has distinguished herself by being responsible for Management Development for LensCrafters Worldwide for ten years, then establishing a successful retail nursery and garden center. She is now a senior consulting partner with the Ken Blanchard Companies. She is recognized as an innovative speaker, most recently partnering with Xilinx, Bellsouth, LensCrafters, General Motors, Marmaxx, American Honda, Amgen, Proctor & Gamble, Genentech, AOL, Merck, KPMG, Pharmacia, Synopsis, and Insurance Agents of America.

Marta studied business and psychology at the University of Louisville and Bellarmine University.

Marta lives in Denver, Colorado, with her husband, Tim, and their Akita, Hana.

Julie Stark is a senior instructional design specialist for the LensCrafters division of Luxottica Retail. She specializes in the design and development of management training solutions for all levels of the organization. With more than ten years of experience consulting to organizations in retail, manufacturing, and public education, Julie seeks a panoramic view of what makes people and processes work well together.

Using strategic methods to uncover growth opportunities in a company, Julie then develops creative systems and training solutions to bring the organization to the next level of success. Julie has designed both facilitator-led and computer-based training in competency areas such as recruiting and selection, coaching, problem solving and analysis, employee recognition, and customer service.

Julie holds an undergraduate degree in education from the University of Michigan and a master of curriculum design from Harvard University. Her current endeavors are supported by a long history working with diverse learners—from at-risk youth in Detroit and non-native speakers of English in Colombia, South America, to graduate-level education students at Eastern Michigan University.

Julie lives with her husband, Steven, and children, Ben and Noah, in Chicago. There she continues to be a life-long learner.

Sarah Caverhill has successfully fused over twenty years of experience in sales, management, and human resources into a career as a sought-after consultant and speaker. Currently she holds the position of director of the East Coast Region for the Ken Blanchard Companies. In this position she uses the many theories and tools she once researched and taught to clients as a consultant. This combination of practical real-world experience and knowledge of cutting-edge theories has created a unique view of what really works in leadership.

As a speaker, Sarah consistently hits the mark with her enthusiastic, innovative presentations. Seminar, workshop, and training audiences learn vital concepts from her in an atmosphere of active discovery. She has devoted her career to helping others succeed in business, whether they are employees, seminar attendees, or people she has mentored.

Sarah began her career with BellSouth and has held positions in sales, leadership, and training. She joined the Ken Blanchard Companies as a senior consulting partner in 1995 and has worked with many different clients, including BellSouth, ALLTel, America Online, Chick-fil-A, J. P. MorganChase, Cingular Wireless, GlaxoSmithKline, and Dr. Pepper/7Up. She holds a master of business administration and has won several regional and national speaking competitions. She lives with her daughter and husband in Atlanta, Georgia.

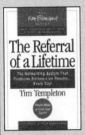